Hop On the Water Cycle

By NADIA HIGGINS

Illustrations by SARA INFANTE

Music by DREW TEMPERANTE

CANTATA
LEARNING

WWW.CANTATALEARNING.COM

CANTATA
LEARNING

Published by Cantata Learning
1710 Roe Crest Drive
North Mankato, MN 56003
www.cantatalearning.com

Library of Congress Control Number: 2017007527
978-1-68410-035-4 (hardcover/CD)
978-1-68410-077-4 (paperback)

Hop On the Water Cycle by Nadia Higgins
Illustrated by Sara Infante
Music by Drew Temperante

Book design, Tim Palin Creative
Editorial direction, Flat Sole Studio
Executive musical production and direction, Elizabeth Draper
Music arranged and produced by Drew Temperante

Printed in the United States of America in North Mankato, Minnesota.
072017   0367CGF17

ACCESS THE MUSIC!

SCAN CODE WITH MOBILE APP

CANTATALEARNING.COM

TIPS TO SUPPORT LITERACY AT HOME

WHY READING AND SINGING WITH YOUR CHILD IS SO IMPORTANT

Daily reading with your child leads to increased academic achievement. Music and songs, specifically rhyming songs, are a fun and easy way to build early literacy and language development. Music skills correlate significantly with both phonological awareness and reading development. Singing helps build vocabulary and speech development. And reading and appreciating music together is a wonderful way to strengthen your relationship.

READ AND SING EVERY DAY!

TIPS FOR USING CANTATA LEARNING BOOKS AND SONGS DURING YOUR DAILY STORY TIME

1. As you sing and read, point out the different words on the page that rhyme. Suggest other words that rhyme.

2. Memorize simple rhymes such as Itsy Bitsy Spider and sing them together. This encourages comprehension skills and early literacy skills.

3. Use the questions in the back of each book to guide your singing and storytelling.

4. Read the included sheet music with your child while you listen to the song. How do the music notes correlate to the words of the song?

5. Sing along on the go and at home. Access music by scanning the QR code on each Cantata book. You can also stream or download the music for free to your computer, smartphone, or mobile device.

Devoting time to daily reading shows that you are available for your child. Together, you are building language, literacy, and listening skills.

Have fun reading and singing!

Water keeps going around and around! This is called the water **cycle**. The water cycle is made up of three steps. **Evaporation** is when water **vapor** rises into the air. **Condensation** is when water droplets gather into clouds. **Precipitation** happens when water falls from the clouds.

Turn the page to learn more about the water cycle. Remember to sing along!

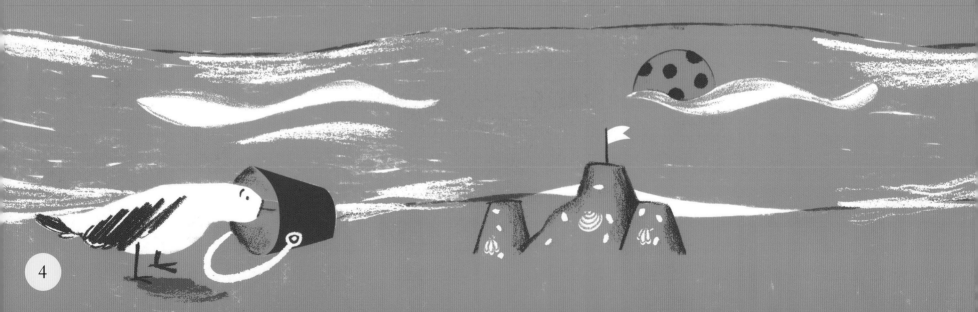

Hop on the water cycle.
It's the wettest ride in town:
water changing, water moving
up and down and all around.

Grab your umbrella. Step right up!

Ready, set, first stop: evaporation!

Shining down, the sun's hot rays
turn water into its **gas** phase.

From oceans, puddles, anything wet,
water vapor floats over your head.

Hop on the water cycle.
It's the wettest ride in town:
water changing, water moving
up and down and all around.

Grab your umbrella. Step right up!

Ready, set, second stop: condensation!

Water vapor on the rise
cools to liquid before your eyes.

Tiny drops form clouds so white,
casting shadows in the sunlight.

13

Hop on the water cycle.
It's the wettest ride in town:
water changing, water moving
up and down and all around.

Grab your umbrella. Step right up!

Ready, set, third stop: precipitation!

In a cloud, drops bump and grow,
oh, so heavy. They cannot float.

Down comes rain and down comes snow.
Back to oceans water flows.

17

Dance stop! Do the water cycle bop!

Evaporation, float your hands in the air.
Condensation, shape clouds in your hair.

Precipitation, bring rain to your feet.
Keep moving with the water cycle beat!

19

Hop on the water cycle.
It's the wettest ride in town:
water changing, water moving
up and down and all around.

20

Hop on the water cycle.
It's the wettest ride in town:
water changing, water moving
up and down and all around.

21

SONG LYRICS
Hop On the Water Cycle

Hop on the water cycle.
It's the wettest ride in town:
water changing, water moving
up and down and all around.
Grab your umbrella. Step right up!

Ready, set, first stop: evaporation!
Shining down, the sun's hot rays
turn water into its gas phase.
From oceans, puddles, anything wet,
water vapor floats over your head.

Hop on the water cycle.
It's the wettest ride in town:
water changing, water moving
up and down and all around.
Grab your umbrella. Step right up!

Ready, set, second stop: condensation!
Water vapor on the rise
cools to liquid before your eyes.
Tiny drops form clouds so white,
casting shadows in the sunlight.

Hop on the water cycle.
It's the wettest ride in town:
water changing, water moving
up and down and all around.
Grab your umbrella. Step right up!

Ready, set, third stop: precipitation!
In a cloud, drops bump and grow,
oh, so, heavy. They cannot float.
Down comes rain and down comes snow.
Back to oceans water flows.

Dance stop! Do the water cycle bop!
Evaporation, float your hands in the air.
Condensation, shape clouds in your hair.
Precipitation, bring rain to your feet.
Keep moving with the water cycle beat!

Hop on the water cycle.
It's the wettest ride in town:
water changing, water moving
up and down and all around.

Hop on the water cycle.
It's the wettest ride in town:
water changing, water moving
up and down and all around.

Hop On the Water Cycle

Hip Hop
Drew Temperante

Verse 2
Ready, set, second stop: condensation!
Water vapor on the rise
cools to liquid before your eyes.
Tiny drops form clouds so white,
casting shadows in the sunlight.

Verse 3
Ready, set, third stop: precipitation!
In a cloud, drops bump and grow,
oh, so, heavy. They cannot float.
Down comes rain and down comes snow.
Back to oceans water flows.

ACCESS THE MUSIC!
SCAN CODE WITH MOBILE APP
CANTATALEARNING.COM

GLOSSARY

condensation—when tiny water droplets gather to form clouds

cycle—a set of things that happen again and again in the same order

evaporation—when water heats up and turns from liquid to water vapor

gas—something that is like air and has no shape

precipitation—when water falls from clouds as snow, rain, hail, or sleet

vapor—something in its gas form that is very small droplets in the air

GUIDED READING ACTIVITIES

1. Think about the water cycle. What parts of the water cycle can you see? What parts can't you see?

2. The three parts of the water cycle are evaporation, condensation, and precipitation. Draw a scene showing one of these parts happening.

3. The water cycle is a series of steps. Think of the things you do every day, such as getting to and from school or going to eat lunch. List all the steps you have to do for one of these things.

TO LEARN MORE

Cannons, Heather Cox. *Rain*. North Mankato, MN: Heinemann-Raintree, 2015.

Olien, Rebecca. *The Water Cycle at Work*. North Mankato, MN: Capstone, 2016.

Paul, Miranda. *Water is Water: A Book About the Water Cycle*. New York, NY: Roaring Brook Press, 2015.

Rustad, Martha E. H. *Water*. North Mankato, MN: Capstone, 2014.